Harley-Davidson

by Julie Wilson

Acknowledgements

Photographs © Newspress

First published in Great Britain by Axis Education Ltd

ISBN 978-1-84618-104-7

Axis Education
PO Box 459
Shrewsbury
SY4 4WZ

Email: enquiries@axiseducation.co.uk

www.axiseducation.co.uk

Printed by The Cromwell Press, Trowbridge, Wiltshire.

The Harley-Davidson legend began in a shed. It was a 10 foot by 15 foot shed in Milwaukee, Wisconsin, USA. In this shed, in 1901, 21-year-old William S Harley made a drawing of an engine that would fit into a bicycle. This engine only had 3 horsepower, but the frame he and his friend Arthur Davidson designed was a loop shape, quite different from anything that was already around. It set the Harley-Davidson apart from any other cycle of its time. Within two years, the shed door had 'Harley-Davidson Motor Company' written on it. William and Arthur had made the first Harley-Davidson motorcycle and Arthur's brother Walter had got in on the act.

This was the result of years of working, dreaming and perfecting drawings of what they thought motorbiking should be about. In 1903, they sold their first motorcycle to a friend and, in 1904, the first Harley-Davidson dealer opened in Chicago. The bike was a racer and, in 1905, the year they took on their first employee, Harley-Davidson won its first race – a 15 mile event in Chicago. William Harley and Arthur Davidson were joined by a third Davidson brother, William in 1907.

The wooden shed was passed over for a small factory in 1906. There were six staff and a catalogue! One year later, they had 18 staff and had made over 150 motorcycles. Harley-Davidson bikes were fast becoming the coolest things on the streets.

They were pretty cool on the track, too. Harleys won several contests in 1908 and also broke speed records. All in all, the company was building a reputation for making really tough motorcycles. They even began to supply the police force with bikes. In 1909, the first Harley-Davidson with 49.5cc and 7 horsepower was brought out.

It was the guys' aunt, Janet Davidson, who came up with the idea of painting a stripe onto the bike instead of leaving it grey. In 1911, the red and black badge, the 'Bar & Shield' logo, was added. It remains the company's emblem to this day.

One of many Harley dealerships.

The story gained a momentum of its own through the next three decades. Harley-Davidson enjoyed success at races, endurance contests and hill climbs. In the end, they formed a Racing Department. 'Team Harley-Davidson' became known as the 'Wrecking Crew' because they were winning just about everything!

By 1914, you could even buy sidecars for these bikes. A year later, the bikes had as many as three gears and were being sold to the American army for use in the First World War. In the end, 20,000 were sold for war work. By 1920, Harley-Davidson was the biggest motorbike maker in the world. You could get them from 2000 dealers in 67 countries. On the track, the Harley was the first bike to ever win a race with a top speed of over 100mph.

During the 1920s, Harley-Davidson suffered from the success of the Model T Ford car, but hung on in there. The bikes got teardrop-shaped fuel tanks in 1925, and front brakes in 1928. In 1929, the 45cc V-twin engine (later to be known as the 'flathead') was introduced on the D model. It was so reliable that it was available on Harley-Davidson motorbikes right up to 1973.

Still racing.

From 1931–1953, the only real competition to Harley-Davidson was the Indian motorbike, made by Hendee Manufacturing. Sales were low during the Great Depression, so the art-deco 'eagle' design was painted on all fuel tanks. This and other graphic designs were brought in to attract more buyers.

When America joined the Second World War in 1941, commercial production was stopped in order to make bikes for the army. By the end of the war, Harley-Davidson had made nearly 90,000 models for military use. However, Harley-Davidson itself was by now a huge company and the making of civilian motorbikes began again at the end of the war in 1945. In 1947, people who went to the yearly dealers' meeting in Milwaukee were taken on a train ride to a 'secret destination'. It turned out to be a new factory. The same year, Harley-Davidson began selling the classic H-D black leather motorcycle jacket.

Look at those pipes!

By 1950, each member of the original Harley-Davidson foursome had died, but the legend lived on. In 1952, the K model was brought out to compete with smaller, sportier motorcycles coming mainly from Great Britain. The K eventually became the Sportster. Hendee Manufacturing went out of business, beginning Harley-Davidson's role as the only US motorcycle maker for the next 46 years. In 1957, a new young star called Elvis Presley posed for the cover of the May Harley-Davidson Enthusiast magazine, sitting on a 1956 model KH.

In 1977, Harley-Davidson introduced the FXS Low Rider. With drag-style handlebars, it lived up to its name by placing the rider in a lower than usual seating position. In 1979 the Fat Bob came out. It was called 'Fat' because it had two fuel tanks. The 'Bob' part came from the 'bobbed' fenders or bumpers (meaning that they had been cut or resized).

Sportster 1200 Low.

These new bikes were popular but did not save Harley-Davidson from hardship in the 1980s. Harley-Davidson had joined with American Machine and Foundry (AMF) when family ownership was a thing of the past. The downside was that they were turning out low-quality bikes far too quickly. It was no surprise when they began to lose out to the cheap Japanese market.

In 1981, AMF put Harley-Davidson up for sale. No one was interested, until, on February 26th 1981, 13 Harley-Davidson managers bought the company. Three years later it showed to the world the 1340cc V^2 Evolution engine on five models, including the all-new Softail. This engine was the result of seven years of work. It was more powerful, cleaner and cooler than other engines. As a testament to the success of the management buyout, Harley-Davidson was listed on the New York Stock Exchange in 1987. A year later, over 60,000 fans celebrated the company's 85th Anniversary in Milwaukee.

Harley was back.

Did it ever go away?

Anniversaries have been a big thing for Harley fans since 1988. The 90th anniversary in 1993 was celebrated with about 100,000 people riding in a parade of motorbikes. In 1998 they celebrated the 95th anniversary with more than 140,000 riders in Milwaukee. More than 250,000 people came to Milwaukee for the 100th Anniversary Celebration and Party in 2003.

Racing had also continued during this time. In 1994, Harley-Davidson entered superbike racing with the introduction of the VR1000 motorbike. It wasn't until 2001, though, that the first female for Team Harley-Davidson was announced – 17 year-old Jennifer Snyder, the first woman to win a national event in the Formula USA National Dirt Track Series!

In 2006, the first of the six-speed transmissions was made available and Harley-Davidson showed its plans for an all new museum in Milwaukee, planned for an opening in 2008. Also in 2006, Harley-Davidson opened the first dealership in China.

Harley has a lot of fans!

Nowadays, Harley-Davidson can't keep up with demand. In fact, there is a two-year waiting list on some models.

There are now five families of Harley-Davidson bikes. They are the Dyna, the Sportster, the Softail, the Touring and the VRSC (V-Rod). They're all Harleys through and through, but each has its own style. The Dyna has a low, laid-back look and the Softail looks like a Harley from the 1930s. The Touring has lots of storage space and is built for long-distance comfort, the V-Rods are power cruisers with hot rod styling and the Sportster is narrower than the other bikes, with two engine choices.

One of the Softail bikes is the Fatboy. This came out in 1990 and is a modern legend of motorbike design. It has been a Harley favourite for many riders. Just take a look – from the thick fork tubes and solo headlight to the floorboards and shotgun pipes, this bike is larger than life! It can carry five gallons of fuel – not as much as some big bikes but still a lot – and it has a 140mm tyre at the front and a 200mm tyre behind. Both are wrapped around 17 inch wheels, made of silver aluminium.

Once you get on it, you'll be laughing all the way to the motorway. Imagine yourself out there, sitting over a huge serving of beautiful chrome, large open spaces all around. You can be sure everyone will see you coming.

You know it's a Fatboy.

The Sportster family has been around since 1957. It was first brought out in order to rival imported bikes. There have been lots of changes, taking nothing away from the passion many riders feel for it. Its model number always began with the letter 'X' as this was the next available letter in the alphabet that Harley had not already used. The first model was known as the Sportster XL. The L is normally given to a model that is one step more powerful. The XL had a right-hand shift, four speeds and full suspension. Its engine had 40 horsepower. It cost $1103! That's £4175 in today's terms.

In 1957, a total of 1983 machines were sold. By 1958, the Sportster XLH model was added, the H showing that this was the second step beyond a basic model. In 1983 came the XLX-61, a black stripped-down model with no other name. It had a solo seat, peanut-shaped tank and one front brake. The XR-750 racing machine appeared in 1970. It won races for over 25 years.

The Evolution Sportster was introduced in 1986. In 1988, the Sportster Hugger package was on offer. This lowered the suspension to a 26 inch seat height – designed to be attractive to women riders. The advertising was never actually aimed at women, though, for fear that men might think of the Sportster as less than manly. Even so, the result is that many still see the Sportster as a women's bike, while at the same time, it is thought to be the 'hot rod' of Harleys!

A Sportster.

There is always a demand for Sportsters. In the year 2005, Sportster sales were 21.3% of all H-D sales. In 2005, Harley-Davidson sold 70,215 of them. The income from all sales between July and September 2006 was $1.64 billion (£863,542,000) and Sportster sales played a big part in this.

In 1988, the XLH-1200 Sportster came out. This is a long, low, street bike with a chromed-out Evolution engine at the centre of its narrow frame. It has 1200cc and the handlebar grips come 250mm closer to the rider than other bikes. Add this to a seat height of only 660mm, a lowered suspension and mid-mount foot controls and you have a machine that feels as good as it looks. It's so much easier to put your feet down with this bike, if you ever want to!

Another bike from the Sportster family is the Harley-Davidson Roadster. This is a bike with lots of options and unique features. The wheels are silver 13-spoke aluminum. Being quite a big bike, it's probably better for taller riders, but the seat can be moved to fit your height and can carry a maximum of 565 pounds. Luckily, the handlebar has a good grip for even the biggest of hands!

In the saddle of a 1200 Roadster, any stretch of road is the place to be. Perhaps this is because the Roadster frame can make an ordinary road feel extraordinary. With its wide, polished handlebar and chrome headlight visor, this is a true Harley!

The Roadster.

Get in the saddle of a Road King and you'll feel at home straight away. It's a bold bike, with huge forks and fenders, a big chrome headlight and footboards that look like platforms. Everything is designed to make your journey one to remember. There is a detachable windshield, weather-resistant, lockable saddlebags and plenty of room for two.

This bike just makes you want to ride. For ever. You could easily spend a day in the saddle and not notice. It has great handling and with a low centre of gravity and good balance, tight turns are easy. It is easy to creep through traffic if you feel like it. You can even leave it in top gear at low speeds! On twisty roads, it leans around curves like a dream. You won't scrape a footboard at any angle. The braking power is awesome, better than you would expect of a tourer.

At around £10,000, it isn't cheap, but it will most likely hold its value like no other bike. On the Road King, you'll get compliments and questions. In fact, expect a lot of drooling. You'll end up feeling that it isn't just the bike that's special. With you on it, you're a double act!

'King of the Road' on a Road King!

Oh... for a Harley!

A Fatboy sculpture.

Modern Harley-Davidsons attract all kinds of views. However, the V-Rod has caused a real stir amongst both bike lovers and non-bike lovers. It's a fantastic bike, a true rival to the Japanese cruiser, and you can see why it gets praise from motorbike riders as well as the media. The sleek aluminium, the bodywork, the sweeping exhaust – all make you want one of these. There may be a whole range of colours to choose from but all roadside watchers will ever see is a blur! That's because the engine has 115 horsepower.

The V-Rod is a big bike yet it moves as if it is weightless. At 275kg, it is certainly lighter than other Harleys. It also has interesting features like removable lower sections to pull the engine out for servicing. In fact, one of the interesting things about this bike is that its design was carried out in complete secrecy. Nobody knew what the result would be. It turned out to be possibly the best and most original new American motorbike ever.

When you see a V-Rod you want to know about it, whether you are a motorbike lover or not. If you're an extrovert who rides a V-Rod, you must be loving all that attention!

A V-Rod in 'X-Men: The Last Stand'.

Blast down the open road on the V-Rod and you'll have a huge smile on your face. Ride it around town and you'll find it handles low speeds like a dream. With a seat height of 660mm it feels very long and very low. The balance, the steering, the low centre of gravity all make it surprisingly easy to handle. Even better, you could fall asleep to the sound it makes – there is no vibration and a beautiful hum comes from massive, curved pipes. And what about how it makes you look? This bike is a real poser!

The hydraulic clutch (Harley's first) is smooth, even with the lightest pull. You may need to work hard on u-turns in the car park, with your foot down and your brain on the matter in hand, but you'll still find the handling wonderful. The switchgear is lovely with chunky, round-edged knobs of black plastic. Get into first and stay there until you're really ready. Then, and only then, hit second and rev it some more. It's sweet. It will talk to you. The engine purrs and you shift effortlessly through the gears enjoying the ride. What's more, you get nearly 50mpg on the road for your efforts.

It's a well thought-out bike. Ignore anybody who says it isn't a real Harley. It is now.

A real Harley!

This V-Rod was auctioned at David Beckham's World Cup party.

Harley-Davidson is not just known for motorbikes. It's known for style, and for lots of famous people, Harley style is the one to be seen with.

Back in 1969, a film called *Easy Rider* made the Harley-Davidson a movie star in its own right. On a less positive note, the Hell's Angels chose the Harley as their mode of transport. When they rolled into town, people locked the doors and pulled the curtains, such was their reputation for trouble. Luckily, the bikes have enjoyed being linked with less shocking personalities, like Arnold Schwarzenegger and Chris Eubank. Even Bill Clinton has posed for photographers on a Harley.

In the non-celebrity world, the typical Harley rider is male, married and over 30 with an above-average income. However, more and more women are turning to them. As a result, there are now more items aimed at women in Harley's range of clothing and accessories. No wonder Tina Turner has been seen on one!

In over 100 years of bike building, the company has learned the importance of good quality riding gear. Harley riding is so popular that this gear has got to be the kind that keeps out the wind, rain and snow. Go out on the road in a Harley-Davidson jacket, helmet, boots and rain suit and you will feel at one with the machine you're riding.

Beyonce tries one out.

The Harley Owners Group was formed in 1983. This was in response to a growing need for riders to share their passion and show their pride. By 1985, membership totalled 60,000. It became known as HOG, and went international in 1991. The first European HOG Rally took place in Cheltenham. At that time, worldwide membership had reached 151,600, with 685 local groups.

Through the 1990s, HOG hysteria spread into Asia. By 1999, worldwide membership had hit the half-million mark. There were 1,157 local groups. Today, there are more than a million members. This makes HOG the largest motorcycle organisation in the world. There are no signs of it slowing down.

HOG hysteria – be part of the crowd.

Why do people love to ride motorbikes? Of course, it's almost impossible to explain. Maybe it's because there are roads and distant towns to discover. Maybe it's because riders have a sense of adventure. Maybe it's just because they can.

Of course, there are practical reasons. Motorbikes can get round the traffic, are generally cheap to run and are easy to park. For the tourer in you, motorbikes take you out into the world instead of keeping you from it. For the cruiser and sports rider, there are the joys of riding, leaning into turns and feeling the engine under them. Riders connect with each other in a way that goes beyond being practical, and many riders attend events and rallies.

The joy of riding ... the joy of leaning ...

Why do people ride Harley-Davidsons? It's a practical option for travel, like all forms of transport, but that's missing the point. A Harley-Davidson can be made to fit any rider. Riders are as passionate about their bike as the ride itself. The curves of the fender, the lines of the fuel tank, the clean reflections from perfect chrome – these set Harley-Davidson motorcycles apart from all others.

The sound of a Harley-Davidson engine makes your heart beat. It thumps the pavement. It's a drug. Your ears get to know a Harley from its sound just as your eyes get to know one from its shape. It's easy to spot a Harley on the horizon.

The Harley-Davidson is so much more than a motorbike. It is a mix of effort, love and achievement. It is an object of raw beauty.

So much more than a motorbike.

Raw beauty.

Technical specification – Harley-Davidson

Make	Harley-Davidson
Model	VRSCA V-Rod
Engine	1131cc
Transmission	6-speed
Frame	Aluminium
Front tyre	120/70 ZR19 (60W)
Rear tyre	180/55 ZR18 (74W)
Length	2435mm
Seat height	660mm
Wheelbase	1710mm
Weight	275kg
Fuel tank capacity	14.0 litres
Maximum power	115hp
Price	£11,995

Glossary

anniversaries	yearly celebrations
art-deco	a style of design from the 1930s
auctioned	sold at auction to the highest bidder
awesome	amazing, fantastic
capacity	how much petrol the engine can hold
catalogue	a book showing items for sale
cc (cubic centimetres)	a measure of engine capacity
civilian	a non-military person
clutch	the part of the car that releases the gears
compete	be in competition with, fight against
cruiser	bike meant for long-distance trips
dealer	a business that sells the bikes for the manufacturer
destination	the place you're going to
drag style	'chopper' style handlebars, that are raised and wide
drool	to want something so bad that you're almost dribbling at the mouth
extrovert	outgoing, confident
fender	bumper, the low frame at the front of the bike
footboard	the platform running along the bike that you can put your feet on
graphic designs	bold and colourful patterns and images
handling	how the bike feels, how it drives
hot rod	a name given to fast and cool-looking bikes

hp	horsepower; a unit of power
hydraulic	powered by water
hysteria	loss of control; uncontrolled crying or laughing
kg (kilogram)	a measure of weight (just over two pounds)
mm (millimetre)	a small measure of length: 10mm = 1cm (centimetre)
perfecting	making perfect
poser	someone who thinks they look really cool; a vain person
reflection	mirror image
reputation	how something is known
sidecar	the small unit for a passenger, attached to the side of a motorbike
suspension	the springs that protect the bike from shocks transmitted through the wheels
switchgear	the parts you turn on a motorbike to change gear
transmission	another word for gearbox
weather-resistant	can protect you in all weathers; weather-proof
wheelbase	the distance between the front and rear wheels